ANYONE WILL TELL YOU

Sibling Rivalry Press, LLC
PO Box 26147
Little Rock, AR 72221

info@siblingrivalrypress.com

www.siblingrivalrypress.com

ISBN: 978-1-943977-91-8

Library of Congress Control No: 2018909384

By special invitation, this title is housed in the Rare Book and Special Collections Vault of the Library of Congress.

First Sibling Rivalry Press Edition, April 2019

Wendy Chin-Tanner

ANYONE WILL TELL YOU

SIBLING RIVALRY PRESS
DISTURB/ENRAPTURE
Little Rock, Arkansas

CONTENTS

I. SOL, OCTO-GRAVIDA

II. WHO'S AFRAID

III. ANYONE WILL TELL YOU

For Tyler, Maddy, and Lucy,
my trinity.

I

SOL, OCTO-GRAVIDA

GATHERING

I awake
before the
final hush

of the night's
lassitude
drains away

thicker than
water and
simplicity

of sunlight
knifed through blinds
why did I

dream about
landed fish
fins flapping

in the dirt
the wings of
flightless birds

so many
useless things
gathering

INDEX

once I had
long black hair

           I confess

that it was
beautiful

           wait this is

a poem
once I had

           beautiful

long hair and
a baby

           I confess

I hungered
wait this is

           a poem

about how
once I had

           a baby

and I was
still hungry

           I confess

I wanted
another

           I confess

I wanted
two babies

                    wait I should

say how I
tried to have

                    another

and it died
I confess

                    I tried for

another
after that

                    I confess

it died in
me too I

                    confess two

babies died
inside me

                    wait let me

tell you once
I cut my

                    long black hair

I confess
that it was

                    beautiful

THE MOTHER IN THIS POEM IS ME OR YOU OR YOUR MOTHER

mother is
a falling
star a bead

of sweat of
blood of bread
our daily

bread on which
we fed the
thread of life

the trouble
and strife of
he you wed

with heart and
head you pledged
in daddy's

bed there is
no rest for
wickedness

lest evil eye
pry babe from
breast again

I rest my
case on wave
and wind hey

knight hey knave
come save me
blame me for

sin of rage
its wage so
high I am

both monster
and slave shame
me slay me

this is the
Labyrinth
where you play

Theseus
and I play
Minotaur

it's okay
it's just a
metaphor

LAPSARIAN

Spring, the first nectarines of the season
      have come but the purple calla lilies

I tucked for winter in the sod have not
      survived, eaten from below by moles. I

try not to take it as a sign: of cradle
      becoming grave, gravid earth gone

suddenly birthless, barren after
      deflowering, devouring. Lapsarian:

I've seen what lies beyond these garden gates.

BEFORE THE FALL

Now that we're in midsummer, my love,
    all the usual flowers are in bloom.

When the foxgloves, trillium, and creeping thyme
    flaunt their blowsy bellies, who notices

the moss that cushions the loam, or the lichen
    that arms the trunks of the pine and fir?

Let's walk through the woods quietly.
    Take my hand in silence, then let me go.

BLUE MOON

After the appointed fuck, I wander
    the house barefoot, climbing up, peering

out every window until I find you
    in the attic skylight to the right

of my desk, your light not blue but milky
    white, filtered through a caul. Your body

is pale, full-bodied, but scarred. You're old,
    I suppose, a sterile rock. I sit

in the dark and watch as we both turn.
    You, a helium balloon whose string tugs

at the fist of a fussy child who might
    look up at the sky and let go.

SUPERMOON

The night abides making the windowpane
        a mirror mirroring my pale face, black hair,

brown eyes. Time normalizes everything,
        even these months and months of nothing,

the colossal space between moons and stars.
        We should be able to bear it, this moon

burning outside the window, yellower,
        leaning closer than ever before,

circling us circling the unseen sun. And in
        the lightless worlds within, a miniature moon

floats in my womb's slippery night,
        heart beating time, time beating heart.

R STANDS FOR

Replication, the act of making
    the second once you've done it once,

thinking you should do it again, thinking
    it begins as all things begin with

the ideation of the thing since you
    know the Real begins with the Symbolic

always, action following thought: Our
    Baby of Best Laid Plans. Hubris. Poof! Dark

magic. *At conception the gamete
    enters a Black Box*, says Dr. C.

*Even with the most painstaking monitoring,
    we never can tell.* Ha! Dr. C belies

without realizing her entire profession,
    without realizing that what she says

is funny: The Black Box That Swallows. My
    Black Box in which nothing can explain why

we can't get one to stick, or how the two
    other unstickings proved that what was bound

could be easily unbound. The truth: for such
    revocations, we have found no restitution

for cancellation or loss, no credit, no
    exchange of goods. No good. No exhortation

can change anything. Resolution lies
  in resignation; this list of rhymes

scribbled on the back of a receipt.

FEMARA

is an oral non-steroidal aromatase
        inhibitor inhibiting estrogen.

Femara is used by male bodybuilders
        to achieve peak muscular tone and by

post-menopausal women to treat breast
        cancer. In pre-menopausal women,

suppression of estrogen tricks
        the adrenals into pumping out more

to goad the ovaries, taunting, plumping,
        primping. No coincidence that the gland

for fight-or-flight is the site of potential
        motherhood. If you tell me I can't, I'll

do it or die trying. I swallow my pills.
        My follicles lay one enormous egg.

Bok Bok Bok means white in Cantonese,
        the color of mourning. Morning

is the best time to test your pee
        and practice the piano. Maybe Bach,

that brutal arithmancy: 37 +
        39 = Infertility.

PORTRAIT

Maddy draws me—

a head,
a pair of boobs,

and beneath, a womb
where the egg,

a speck of black pen, lays.

SOL, OCTO-GRAVIDA

other stars
glance askance
at your hot

gaseous flesh
wobbling as
your planets

spin around
tugging at
your center

gravity's
apron strings
tether just

tight enough
to hold us
together

II

WHO'S AFRAID

AT SEA

She was a storyteller and you believed
        the sofa was your little boat, fishing,

the smoke-stained ceiling lifting all at once
        to a storming sky, the worn brown carpet

a churning, shark-infested sea. The unwashed
        window was, she said, the eye of the storm

seeing everything. You could see
        the water, the rain, the mast, the yawl you steered

frantically, turning the wheel. You believed
        the rations had fallen into the waves

as you were rocked and overturned, and that
        from the wreckage only one of you could return.

AND NOT LOOK AWAY (BROOKLYN, 1985)

The pale green of the trees standing before
the crumbling brownstone all June. Later,

their leaves would darken in the leaden heat
and the asphalt would soften and return

to tar under the sun's sorrowful gaze.
Mornings, the sidewalk would begin the day

gray, wet from the super's hose. By noon it
would be baked so that the cement glittered,

gleaming like shattered glass. The world seemed to
die each afternoon and nothing ever

happened and nothing ever moved, not air,
not cigarette smoke, not the water

that held the china girl afloat in my
room, black hair, silk robe, and cut sleeves flowing

elegantly, drowning, entombed beneath
a dusty plastic globe. At the kitchen

table, the women sat saying the same
things over and over so that their words

began to rhyme and sound like song. In dreams,
I held my head under until the surface

grew still, and all I could do was make
my eyes see and not blink, and not look away.

WHO'S AFRAID

who is the
wolf at the
table who

pretends there
is no wolf
who's afraid

of the wolf
who eats at
the table

NOT WEEPING BUT FERAL

suspended
where the night
rolls before

us and the
afternoon
scrolls behind

eye through a
telescope
bent backwards

turning in
faint sickle
sweeps feebly

turning to
nostalgia
not weeping

but feral
terrible
but alive

PARENT

Not pomegranate, but
persimmon,

spotted, so easily
bruised, a child's finger-

nail could pierce you through.

ON TRUTH IN A NONMORAL SENSE

In sociology, we say mapping,
> we say cartography instead

of understanding. To profess
> to understand, you see, is hubris.

I am a professional digger. I
> should say excavation or archeology

instead of digging for the truth,
> which is uncouth. Which is emotional.

And, again, hubris. We should never say
> truth. What is the truth, anyway? Instead,

we should say subjectivity, as in: To what
> are we subjected? Or: What is the subject

of the story of your life? To name it,
> I say loss, I say yearn, I say tell me.

What else can I say? In fall, before
> the surgery, we walked, the sky the color

of pigeons. I listened to you breathe, the soft
> wheezing. I listened to the sound of your shoes

shuffling, crunching dead leaves into the ground.
> I thought I would lose you. How could I betray

you by mapping these cities so far away:
> Paris, Prague, Vienna, Kiev? How could

they hurt us? These faint cartographies
      drawn in traces of my DNA, and names,

the names escaping me over time and sea
      poetically in slant, half, off, and straight

rhymes. I could never escape you. Before
us, our name stands constant, and the City stands

constantly shifting, like truth. Like words and meaning,
      making meaningless the crude facts of my making.

[Truth is] a mobile army of metaphors, metonyms, and anthropomorphisms—in short, a sum of human relations which have been enhanced, transposed, and embellished poetically and rhetorically, and which after long use seem firm, canonical, and obligatory (Frederich Nietzsche, On Truth and Lies in a Nonmoral Sense, 1873).

ON TRUTH IN A MORAL SENSE

bury it
say it lies
let it die

before it
reaches the
Rhine finding

traces of train
tracks cattle
cars tattoos

o pater
o pater
noster jus

soli jus
sanguinis
o strange song

VELLEITY

because life
began in
      the sea death

  seems natural
on the beach
      the waves call

    the names
of the dead
       velella

    velella
by-the-wind
      sailors sea

     rafts blue sails
beached by the
      billions a

     bright blue whale
exploded
       fractally

     the fault of
nobody
       not you or

     me or the
inscrutable
        pacific

     this is what
happens when
       you are born

        with a sail
set in one
direction

                                        see the sea
                                        connects the
                        continents

                                    by water
                                    salty as
                    red and those

                                soft bodies
                                seep venom
                onto skin

                                if touched for
                                nothing is
            innocent

                            not tangled
                            seaweeds named
            green rope or

                        wireweed or
                        bladderwrack
        or hiding

                        in the blades
                        trapping prey
    pray do you

                    believe in
                    prayer there
    in books in

                    genetic
                    epistem-
ology

        scraping my
        inner cheeks
                    bloodletting

I'm testing
testing one
       two three is

this poem
a poem
       about me

   or the sea
   you see how
       I always

    place myself
    back at the
       center I

     myself am
     the center
       my self the

      middle king-
      dom of this
       poem I

      must insist
      queen of the
       jellyfish

ON THE OREGON COAST IN FALL

You gather a bucketful of seashells
      shaped like ears, whorled tender cochlea. Hour

by hour, the sea yields feast and famine
      simultaneously: clusters of agates

and fields of shattered crab carcasses. You
      follow a stream strewn with agates—rough, hewn

from sandstone cliffs that give them up more easily
      than basalt bluffs. Gleaming, they lure you on

and on. But plain black rocks will also shine
      when wet. And sand fleas swarm balletically over

the dead at the water's edge, licking clean
      the innards of abandoned shells. Are they

not beautiful? A shell is most valuable
      in the fast-fading time between the death

of the animal inside and the crushing
      blows of the tide rolling into itself.

HOW IT IS WRITTEN

            the cuckoo
in the nest
has got a

big mouth a
            beehive like
a buzz in

            the body
of the things

            left unsaid

say it this
is how it

            is written

BUTTERFLY

We used a butterfly net to catch the great
     green bottle flies that proliferated

down on the ground floor where we sat sweating
     in summer. Swishing a deft wrist first left

then right, my final downward flick trapped
     a hairy, buzzing beast on a flat surface—

the floor, the wall, or the Formica
     countertop. It would lift itself then and

try to fly, frantic for escape from the fine
     gray mesh, but I tightened a fist to make

a smaller cage, a bubble of net,
     and took it to the sink where under the spray

it would drop and shrink. Wasn't it less cruel
     than squishing it with a flip-flop, smearing

its iridescent guts everywhere
     underfoot? Wasn't it better to pretend

it wasn't dead, just sleeping, limp and wet,
     nestled there with the rest of the trash?

DEAD OF WINTER

The jar of
honey on
the window-

sill catches
nothing next

to it a
ladybug
lies supine

legs and wings
folded a

tightly furled
bud morning
rose for it

was winter

ADVENT

ever green
who waits four
Sundays for

the end of
the year clear
brisk air of

night the moon
a small ball
in passing

empurpling
a stripe of
vaulted black

sky a wreath
of the sun's
shadow light

reflection
of a star
you are dust

the dust you
tell yourself
of some dead

star staring
back to see
how far you

have fallen

THE LONG NAP

ends with a nightmare light. At the high window
       overlooking Squibb Hill, I lift my shirt,

press my small round belly against cold
       glass and look. The Watchtower blinks back

the seconds as children play in snow,
       action figures silhouetted below

a horrible crimson sky. I see
       their open mouths as they swirl round and round

on trash can lids all the way down, silent
       in the whooshing din of the BQE.

I dig the heels of my hands into my eyes:
       pinpricks of light, glowing nebulae.

WILLOW

Willow Street
had only
one willow

at the bad
end of the
block I lived

at number
One Willow
Street where the

BQE's
sea sound shook
the house that's

no longer
the house is
only a

house the gate
a gate I
tell myself

the city
is only
a city

MERCURY IN VIRGO

night devours
sleep the hours
surfeited

glut drenched time
sweat slick skin
sheet metal

rainwater
shine I walk
widdershins

warding off
terrors thought
crimes later

at the end
of a dream
the stars in

a cloudless
sky form a
filigree

above a
skein of swans
honk and echo

fragments of
the past its
light can still

prick stinging
rapidly
moving eyes

APOIDEA

"Where the bee sucks, there suck I:
In a cowslip's bell I lie."
          – William Shakespeare, *The Tempest*

Honeybee, hornet, yellowjacket, wasp.
       Cleopatra holds asp to breast: hive loss.

Queen bee. Queen cell. The Queen is in her cups.
       Brother, Caesar, Antony: worthless fucks.

Though woman, lover, other, boss, the hive
       Without its matriarch, like Empire, dies.

III

ANYONE WILL TELL YOU

THREE DISCRETE THOUGH NOT ENTIRELY SEPARATE THOUGHTS

1.

though not thought
now suggests
a later

that's different
past asks to
be present

2.

not even
solitude
lives alone

for even
silence speaks
to someone

3.

to live my
life inside
this walnut

shell I have
painted its
walls in gold

AGATE BEACH

The traveler need not journey on.
    The traveler's journey is one of return.

If not agates, then barnacles, if not
    sweet-smelling seaweed, then shattered shells.
        The traveler need not journey on.

If not mussels, then sea glass, if not

smooth surfaces, then rocks pocked by anemones.
    The traveler's journey is one of return.
        A dead Dungeness crab bobs in the spume.

Waterlogged, it still rises and falls.

The traveler's journey is one of return.
    The traveler need not journey on.

In a tidal pool, an orange sea star
    supplies a sun for another sky.
        The traveler's journey is one of return.

We rinse the sand from our souvenirs

and lose half the agates in our hands.
    The traveler need not journey on.
        We take what we can, rain boots filled

with rocks and shells. We carry our wet socks.

The traveler need not journey on.
    The traveler's journey is one of return.

EIGHT

thunderheads
sumac red
bursting black

dividing
sky last night
she laid her

burning head
in the dip
between my

hip and rib
somnolent
returning

CHILD

I am
the grape;

you are
the wine:

crush me.

THE THIN VEIL

belly up

but not in
death the knife's
edge between

you and she
and labor's
end lies at

the thin veil
you push through
on your back

when she comes

THIS BED THIS ROOM

hourglass sands
scratch skin of
night the thin

scrim between
dark and dawn
flight of bat

wings meadow
lark songs shark
fins slice moon

moving scythe
to spoon round
this bed this

room round clock
measuring
tide and rest

starfish on
sand her splayed
hand my breast

FILIGREE

Orion's

           bright daughter

Capella

           visible

now Chiron's

           in Pisces

full circle
of winter

           stars again

circling it

           will not stop

breath of wood

leaf rot rock

           the rushing

water cold

           wisps of day

light cobwebs

           in her hair

PRELUDE

second week
of the new
year Christmas

lights still lit
on the porch
I walk the

bedtime walk
in the dark
corridor

back and forth
past my pa-
pa playing

piano
piani-
ssimo as

the baby
babbles he
smiles without

looking up
I say I
liked that song

PERSEID

Medusa
music class
fourth grade I

composed her
a song on
glockenspiels

teasing I
called Mama
Medusa

a female
monster she
did not know

about her
life before
that she was

a woman
before she
did not know

betrayal
beheading
meteors

KNOT

worry it
rub it raw
the shawl of

memory
lifts over
grandmother's

gua xia pale
jade lozenge
scraping back

and flat breast-
bone to break
fever it

must bloom a
poppy field
over snow

milk turned to
seed swollen
pearl breaking

ON THE WALL

daughters let
my eye and
later its

memory
hold up a
mirror to

your beauty

AS VENUS STATIONS RETROGRADE

        silver moon
sliver spoon
kindness of

slow summer
dawn who blooms
        unfurling

susurrus
        shredding night
shedding dark-

ness rising
        up she stares
at mother's

face great dark
sky her skin
        flecked with stars

MILKY WAY

hour fallen into
hour day into night into
day suddenly fall

WHEN SLEEPLESS

injunction
              first throb of
fall pines last

berries sweet
              breath of green
trees breathing

indigo
              shadows fade
to gray by

decrements
              can you hear
me when I

don't speak when
              sleepless wind
shredded clouds

show us streaks
              of starlit
sky cirrus

rending drenched
              restless edge
rustles creaks

rushing you
              close your eyes
unhearing

sigh of night
              ground swallows
dark rising

HOW THE SEA

woe woven
we are rain
wet wool weight

and weft we
wait for no
one waiting

for wreck the
rocks break no
matter what

they say you
don't know what
you don't know

how do you
do this how
do you show

me myself
long past due
the distance

between us
the distance
between two

seas I see
it clearly
tonight the

mirror through
the window
the gloom of

the year its
gloaming gleams
of glitter

the stars a
streak ribbon
of silver

the river
you see how
it runs to

the sea you
see how the
sea too is

a mirror

ANYONE WILL TELL YOU

nearly night
the sky bleached
        to winter

        white over
        black water
        sough of wind
        from box fans
        speaking tongues
to the heat

of bodies
of beds and
        rooms rising

        twice the moon
        rose this month
        twice I spoke
        platitudes
        on time and
the color

blue outside
the vault of
        sky dark blue

        violet blushed
        bruised violent
        there's never
        only one
        anyone
will tell you

skin of dust
on liquid
      dusk covered

      I fall and
      fallen thus
      after fall
      it will be
      the middle
of my life

one of those
days become
      one of these

THE CARAVAN

by cobweb
and shadow
dusk colors

drain from the
light greens to
lavenders

purples to
black wings of
dark gliding

past day all
its little
deaths barking

dogs calling
coyotes
calling back

ACKNOWLEDGMENTS

Grateful acknowledgment is made to the following publications where these poems or earlier versions first appeared:

Ampersand Review: "Gathering"
The Margins: "Index" and "Agate Beach"
The Rumpus: "The Mother in This Poem Is Me or You or Your Mother"
Dusie: "Lapsarian," "Femara," and "Eight"
Moonsick Magazine: "Before the Fall" and "Knot"
Ink Node: "Blue Moon" and "Dead of Winter"
The Normal School: "Supermoon," "Apoidea," and "The Thin Veil"
Tinderbox Poetry Journal: "R Stands for"
The Account: "Portrait," "Parent," "Mercury in Virgo," and "And Not Look Away (Brooklyn, 1986)"
Horse Less Review: "Sol, Octo-Gravida," "Perseid," "How the Sea," and "When Sleepless"
Softblow Anthology: "Who's Afraid"
Vinyl Poetry: "On Truth in a Nonmoral Sense" and "Advent"
Gramma Poetry: "Velleity," "Milky Way," "Three Discrete Though Not Entirely Separate Thoughts," and "Child"
Bear Review: "How It Is Written" and "Willow"
Mead: "On the Oregon Coast in Fall"
Angle Poetry Journal: "At Sea" and "Butterfly"
RHINO Poetry: "The Long Nap"
The Collagist: "This Bed This Room"
Atticus Review: "Prelude," and "The Caravan"
Apogee: "Anyone Will Tell You"
North Dakota Quarterly: "Filigree" and "As Venus Stations Retrograde"
Drunk in a Midnight Choir: "Not Weeping but Feral" and "On Truth in a Moral Sense"
Footbridge Above the Falls (Rose Alley Press): "Before the Fall," On the Oregon Coast in Fall," and "How the Sea"
Topophrenia: Place, Narrative, and the Spatial Imagination (Indiana University Press): "On Truth in a Nonmoral Sense"

ABOUT THE AUTHOR

Wendy Chin-Tanner is the author of the poetry collection *Turn* (Sibling Rivalry Press, 2014), which was a finalist for the Oregon Book Award, and co-author of the graphic novel *American Terrorist* (A Wave Blue World, 2012). She is a founding editor at *Kin Poetry Journal*, poetry editor at *The Nervous Breakdown*, and co-founder of A Wave Blue World, an independent publishing company for graphic novels. Wendy is a trained sociologist specializing in race, identity, discourse analysis, and culture, and continues to write and educate on these topics as well as poetry. Born and raised in New York City and educated at Cambridge University, UK, Wendy is the mother of two daughters and the proud daughter of immigrants.

ABOUT THE PRESS

Sibling Rivalry Press is an independent press based in Little Rock, Arkansas. It is a sponsored project of Fractured Atlas, a nonprofit arts service organization. Contributions to support the operations of Sibling Rivalry Press are tax-deductible to the extent permitted by law, and your donations will directly assist in the publication of work that disturbs and enraptures. To contribute to the publication of more books like this one, please visit our website and click *donate*.

Sibling Rivalry Press gratefully acknowledges the following donors, without whom this book would not be possible:

Tony Taylor	Russell Bunge
Mollie Lacy	Joe Pan & Brooklyn Arts Press
Karline Tierney	Carl Lavigne
Maureen Seaton	Karen Hayes
Travis Lau	J. Andrew Goodman
Michael Broder & Indolent Books	Diane Greene
Robert Petersen	W. Stephen Breedlove
Jennifer Armour	Ed Madden
Alana Smoot	Rob Jacques
Paul Romero	Erik Schuckers
Julie R. Enszer	Sugar le Fae
Clayton Blackstock	John Bateman
Tess Wilmans-Higgins & Jeff Higgins	Elizabeth Ahl
Sarah Browning	Risa Denenberg
Tina Bradley	Ron Mohring & Seven Kitchens Press
Kai Coggin	Guy Choate & Argenta Reading Series
Queer Arts Arkansas	Guy Traiber
Jim Cory	Don Cellini
Craig Cotter	John Bateman
Hugh Tipping	Gustavo Hernandez
Mark Ward	Anonymous (12)

www.ingramcontent.com/pod-product-compliance
Lightning Source LLC
Chambersburg PA
CBHW022040090426
42741CB00007B/1136